The Comforter

The Living Presence of Jesus Inside You

by:

Marjie Schaefer

Flourish Through the Word is a community of women of all ages who gather weekly to worship, pray, study the Bible together, and build relationships. From these weekly gatherings, women are then equipped to move out into their arenas of influence and be a light for Jesus.

Flourish is a 501C3 ministry that is supported by the material fees charged for the studies and private donations. If you'd like to find out more about the ministry or make a tax-deductible donation, please visit *flourishthroughtheword.com*. Donations can be made online or by mailing a check to:

Flourish Through the Word
2020 Maltby Rd, PMB 240
Bothell WA 98021

On our website are various Bible study teaching sessions based on the studies our community has done together. These are easily viewed for use in home, church, or small group. Please contact our ministry for more details.

ISBN: 979-8-9909136-0-8

Before you begin...

The content of this five-week study is focused entirely on the Holy Spirit and His ever-present work and presence in the life of the believer.

When the Lord prompted me to spend an entire Bible study season on the Holy Spirit, I initially mapped out an outline of the content, and then prayerfully went to work. The Lord shifted me in a totally different direction, and what you will see as you do this study, is the lingering time spent in John chapters 14, 15, and 16.

This is the conversation Jesus had with His disciples before He was crucified, resurrected, and departed earth.

I pray you will be blessed and encouraged as you spend the next few weeks unpacking this incredible section of scripture and meditating on the actual words of Jesus.

Here's what you need to know as you start:

Each week begins with a hymn, or a worship song reflecting the Holy Spirit. Take the time to personally worship by finding each song on YouTube or Spotify.

Commentary for many of the actual study questions is provided for you each day, and it is very important to read all of it as you proceed and unpack the scriptures.

The purpose of Bible study is not simply to understand profound truths, but to get to know our Heavenly Father better and to draw closer to Jesus. He even told us this exact thing in John 16:25: ***"I will tell you plainly about the Father."***

If our reading and study falls short of not growing closer to the Father it can do more harm than good.

Most days of study end with the opportunity for you to respond in personal prayer based on what you've gleaned from that day of digging into the Word. Prayer is so important!

I've included three additional prayers for you entitled, *Blessing your spirit*. These are taken from a separate book listed in the works cited and are reflective of the content studied that day.

May God bless your study of Him and His precious Holy Spirit,

Dedication

I lovingly dedicate this study to my friends and long-time faithful Bible study leaders,

Teri Bachelor

and

Trisha Baker

These dear friends know the Comforter and long for others to know Him too.

They have both blessed my life immensely.

The Comforter

Week One

Holy, Holy, Holy

Holy, holy, holy! Lord God Almighty!
Early in the morning our song shall rise to Thee;
Holy, holy, holy, merciful and mighty!
God in three Persons, blessed Trinity!

Holy, holy, holy! All the saints adore Thee,
Casting down their golden crowns around the glassy sea;
Cherubim and seraphim falling down before Thee,
Who was, and is, and evermore shall be.

Holy, holy, holy! Though the darkness hide Thee,
Though the eye of sinful man Thy glory may not see;
Only Thou art holy; there is none beside Thee,
Perfect in pow'r, in love, and purity.

Holy, holy, holy! Lord God Almighty!
All Thy works shall praise Thy Name, in earth, and sky, and sea;
Holy, holy, holy; merciful and mighty!
God in three Persons, blessed Trinity!

John B. Dykes, 1861, Public Domain

What is the secret to walking in victory?

It is the presence and power of the Holy Spirit of God in our lives.

Jesus prepared His disciples for His earthly departure and spent a lot of time (three chapters worth!) explaining things to them and getting them ready for the inevitable.

Your Bible study assignment for today is to read. These foundational passages are important to your study ahead.

Pray before you read:

- John 14:1-31

- John 15:1-27

- John 16:1-33

Take your time as you read each passage. Underline anything that stands out to you in your Bible or record any verses here or in your personal journal.

Jesus told the disciples in John 13:33 that He was going to leave them. The disciples wondered where He was going and if they could go with Him. Their minds were full of perplexing questions, and their hearts were burdened at the thought of Jesus no longer being with them.

1. Read **John 14:1-6** to answer the questions. How did Jesus comfort His disciples? Where did He tell them He was going? Did He make a promise to return? How did Jesus tell the disciples they could get to where He was going? Write out verse 6 as you answer.

2. Read John 14:7-11 to answer the questions. None of us have to wait until we enter heaven to know the Father. We can know Him today and receive the spiritual resources we need to keep going no matter our circumstances. What does it mean to know the Father? How did Philip miss the gist of what Jesus was saying? What does Jesus say to the disciples that is of utmost importance (vv. 11-12) to us today?

3. In John 14:12-15, Jesus reveals the privilege of prayer. What are the three aspects of faith from these verses that Jesus outlined for us to follow? *Finish today's study with a prayer of your own, confessing your own belief in Jesus, and asking Him to increase your faith for the study ahead.*

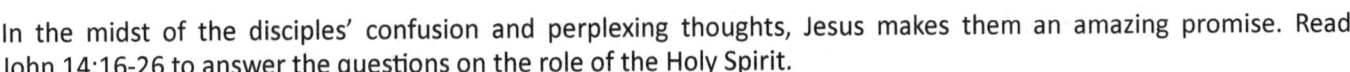

In the midst of the disciples' confusion and perplexing thoughts, Jesus makes them an amazing promise. Read John 14:16-26 to answer the questions on the role of the Holy Spirit.

1. What did Jesus say He would ask (pray) the Father to give to the disciples?

    It was obvious to the disciples that this 'Comforter" was not a regular person they would be able to see, hear, or touch. This is why Jesus was very careful to use key words when He spoke to them about the coming of the Holy Spirit, the 'Comforter'.

    Jesus used the word *'another'* in this verse. This Greek word could be translated: *"I will pray to the Father, and He will send you Someone who is just like Me in every way. He will be identical to Me in the way I speak, the way I think, the way I operate, the way I see things, and the way I do things. When He is present, it will be just as if I am present because we think, behave, and operate the same"* (Renner; pg. 45).

    To understand exactly what Jesus was saying, write out each verse:

    *   John 14:9

    *   Hebrews 1:3

2. As Jesus taught the disciples about the Holy Spirit, He used the Greek word, ***allos—one of the very same kind.*** Jesus is the perfect imprint and very image of the Father's nature. The word ***allos*** reveals that the Holy Spirit perfectly represents the life and nature of Jesus Christ. How do these truths impact you in your relationship with the Holy Spirit?

3. Read: John 14:16 and 26; John 15:26, and John 16:7. What is very evident in the Holy Spirit's ministry in our lives? Write out your favorite verse from these selections here:

4. Write out your **personal prayer** here and incorporate what you have learned today about the Holy Spirit's ministry of comfort in your life.

The Holy Spirit is given two special names by Jesus: 'another Comforter' and 'the Spirit of Truth'.

Our study for the next two days will have us focus on the deeper meaning of the *Comforter.*

Our English word *comfort* comes from two Latin words meaning 'with strength'. We usually think of comfort as soothing someone who is hurting or grieving, but true comfort strengthens us to face life bravely and to keep moving forward, persevering as we do. Some translations call the Holy Spirit 'the Encourager', and this is another great aspect of understanding the work of the Holy Spirit in our lives.

1. The Greek word translated 'Comforter' is ***parakletos*** and it means 'called alongside to assist'. Look up these verses and write out what you learn about the Holy Spirit from each one:

   - John 14:16

   - John 14:26

   - John 15:26

   - John 16:7

   - 1 John 2:1

2. What does the word 'comfort' mean to you? Write out your testimony of how the Holy Spirit has comforted (strengthened, assisted) you in the recent past.

3. As stated above, the Greek compound word ***parakletos*** (translated Comforter) is made up of the words ***para*** and ***kaleo***. The word para simply means alongside and carries the idea of proximity or geographical location. It means being very close to someone. How does knowing the deeper meaning of the word, Comforter, impact your understanding of relating to the Holy Spirit? Write out your thoughtful answer here, knowing there is nothing distant about His relationship with you.

4. Look up Ephesians 1:13 and write what happens to us at the moment of salvation.

5. Use this space to write out your personal prayer of gratitude to the Holy Spirit for His presence, comfort, strength, and closeness in your life.

Today we will be studying the second part of the word *parakletos* (translated Comforter) which is *kaleo.*

Kaleo means to beckon or to call. This is not a verbal communication of someone yelling or calling out, but rather, it is a calling with purpose, intent, and a sense of direction.

1. Look up the following scriptures (each one is so important) and write out what God calls people to based on the use of the word *kaleo* in each of these passages:

    • Matthew 9:13

    • Romans 1:1

    • Romans 8:30

    • Romans 9:11; 24

    • 1 Corinthians 1:9

    • 1 Corinthians 7:15

    • Ephesians 4:1, 4

    • 1 Thessalonians 2:12

    • Hebrews 9:15

- 1 Peter 1:15

- 1 Peter 2:9

2. **The call (*kaleo*)** is always something that points to specific intent. The call of God, through the enabling presence of the Holy Spirit, gives individual insight into the purposes, plans, and design for your life in Christ. Knowing God's call upon your life can change everything about the way you live, what you give your time to, and who you spend your time with. Based on your study this week and in particular, of these scriptures above, what do you sense the Father has called/purposed/destined you to do and to be? Write out your answer here.

3. As you wrap up this initial week on the Holy Spirit, go back through each day's study homework and prayerfully reflect on what you have gleaned from your time spent in God's Word. Review your prayers and potentially, re-voice them to the Lord. Read aloud any verses that spoke powerfully to you. Go back and finish anything you did not complete. Once you've done this 'heart review', **write out a prayer** here and commit your continued study to God.

Blessing Your Spirit

Take the time to pray through this blessing prayer taken from the book, <u>Blessing Your Spirit</u>, by Sylvia Gunter. Fill your name in the blank provided.

_____, listen with your spirit to God's promise in His Word. "For we are God's workmanship, created in Christ Jesus to do good works, which God prepared in advance for us to do" (Ephesians 2:10). Your Father has a purpose for you. I bless you with knowing your purpose as God has seen it in His Heart. I bless you with everything that God has designed you to be, because as you experience the joy of fulfilling your purpose, you will benefit, others will benefit, and the world will be blessed.

_____, I bless you with fulfilling the call of God on your life and living out the fullness of His will. I bless you with being in your Father's time, not running ahead and not lagging behind, but knowing His will and doing His will in the right time, the right place, and the right way, with the right people alongside you.

I bless you with being able to carry out God's work with honor, with peace, with joy, doing God's work, God's way.

I bless you with a life-giving community to fit into. You have a piece to put into a mosaic, and I bless you with fitting together with other people, because you can't do what God has called you to do alone.

I bless you with finding like-hearted, like-visioned, like-spirited others. I bless you with being a part of a family of ministry where you can enjoy your greatest fulfillment as you fit with other people who are finding their fulfillment in God's purposes, and each of you is doing what God has designed you to do.

Your Father will bless you with open doors to walk forward in His time, in His calling, for you to experience the joy of fulfillment of being everything He has called you to be at the right time and in the right place.

Your Father intends for you to have beauty of spirit. I bless you with fulfillment, grace, elegance, and the wisdom and beauty of heaven. You are God's craftsmanship, His masterpiece, His poem. You are not just a piece of a puzzle.

Your Father intends for you to carry the fragrance of heaven, for people to be attracted to you because you have the perfume of heaven.

I bless you _____, with being a fragrant offering as you do the work God wants you to do. I bless you in the Name of Jesus.

The Comforter

Week Two

King of Kings

In the darkness we were waiting
Without hope, without light
'Til from Heaven You came running
There was mercy in Your eyes
To fulfill the law and prophets
To a virgin came the word
From a throne of endless glory
To a cradle in the dirt

Praise the Father, praise the Son
Praise the Spirit, three in one
God of glory, Majesty
Praise forever to the King of Kings

To reveal the kingdom coming
And to reconcile the lost
To redeem the whole creation
You did not despise the cross
For even in your suffering
You saw to the other side
Knowing this was our salvation
Jesus for our sake you died

Praise the Father, praise the Son
Praise the Spirit, three in one
God of glory, Majesty
Praise forever to the King of Kings

And the morning that You rose
All of Heaven held its breath
'Til that stone was moved for good
For the Lamb had conquered death
And the dead rose from their tombs
And the angels stood in awe
For the souls of all who'd come
To the Father are restored

And the church of Christ was born
Then the Spirit lit the flame
Now this gospel truth of old
Shall not kneel, shall not faint
By His blood and in His name
In His freedom I am free
For the love of Jesus Christ
Who has resurrected me

Songwriters: Jason Ingram, Scott Ligertwood, Brooke Gabrielle Fraser.
For non-commercial use only. Data From: Musixmatch

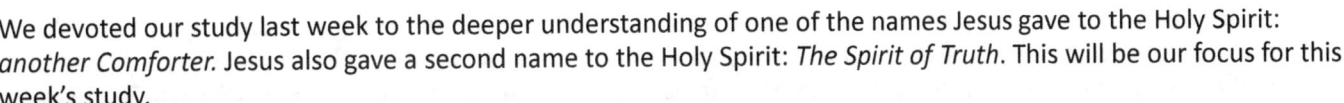

We devoted our study last week to the deeper understanding of one of the names Jesus gave to the Holy Spirit: *another Comforter.* Jesus also gave a second name to the Holy Spirit: *The Spirit of Truth.* This will be our focus for this week's study.

1. Read John 14:16-31. Write out John 14:17 and explain what this verse means to you in your daily life.

2. Look up John 14:6 and John 17:17 and tell how the Spirit of Truth is an embodiment of these two verses. Are there many ways to get to God? Why or why not?

3. The Spirit of Truth uses the Word of truth to guide us into the will and the work of God. Write out each of the verses below and compare the message of Ephesians with the message in Colossians. Tell how both passages describe the same kind of Christian life.

    •   Ephesians 5:18

    •   Ephesians 6:9

    •   Colossians 3:16

    •   Colossians 4:1

4. Summarize your studies from this day in the form of a **prayer**.

As 'the Spirit of Truth', the Holy Spirit is related to Jesus, the Truth, and the Word of God. The Spirit inspired the Word and He also illumines the Word as we read it. This is so we may understand it. Since He is the 'Spirit of Truth', the Holy Spirit cannot lie or be associated with lies. He never leads us to do anything contrary to the Word of God because God's Word is truth. If we want the Holy Spirit to work in our lives, we must make much of the Word of God.

1. How are you currently making much of the Word of God in your daily life? Does the Word of God take priority in your life over everything else you read and devote your time to? Do you feel that this year you have made progress in your personal time of reading the Word? Why or why not? Do you have a plan for your own time in the Word? This is a personal question that requires your time and reflection in prayer. Write down your honest answers here and be sure and end this time of reflection in a **transparent time of conversation with the Lord.**

2. Read John 14:17-21. Why can't the world receive the Holy Spirit? Use other biblical references to explain your answer.

3. Jesus was preparing His disciples for His departure from the earth. As He addressed their fears, Jesus promised them in John 14:18, "I will not leave you as orphans." This word is taken from the Greek word *orphanos*, where we get the word orphan. Write out a description of an orphan and tell how Jesus has promised to be the exact opposite of an orphan through the presence of the Holy Spirit. Use your previous study from Week One to help you answer.

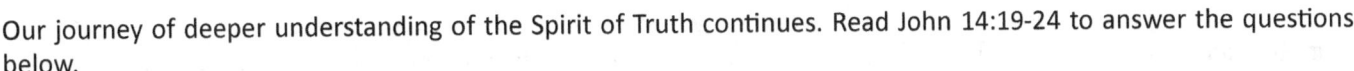

Our journey of deeper understanding of the Spirit of Truth continues. Read John 14:19-24 to answer the questions below.

1. John 14:19 focuses on Jesus' resurrection and post-resurrection appearances to His disciples and other believers. What did He mean by the words He spoke in this verse? How would we see Him and live in Him if He was gone from the earth? (Use John 14:17 to help you answer.)

2. What 'day' was Jesus mentioning in verse 20? Use Acts 2:1-4 to answer.

3. Write out John 14:21 and circle the word love. What is significant about the number of times Jesus spoke of love in this verse? What is the over-arching lesson you glean from this?

4. How does this passage prioritize the "Spirit of Truth"? What have you gleaned from these short verses how the love of the Word, prayer, and obedience facilitates a deeper relationship with the Holy Spirit?

5. Close out your time of study today in a **time of prayer**, recommitting yourself to a renewed love of the Word of God.

When you are born again, the Spirit immediately enters your body and bears witness that you are a child of God. The Spirit is resident, close in proximity, speaks, guides, encourages, helps, and empowers you for the tasks God has called you to do for Him.

As you yield continually to the Father, love the Word, pray, and obey, there is a deeper relationship with the Father, Son, and Holy Spirit

1. Read John 14:16-24 again.

> Jesus said, "***And I will ask the Father, and He will give you another Helper (Comforter, Advocate, Intercessor, Counselor, Strengthener, Standby), to be with you forever***" John 14:14 AMP).

Write how this verse ministers to you in a fresh way after your study of the Holy Spirit so far.

2. From your prayerful reading, summarize each of the eight verses (John 14:16-24) that reveal what you have learned about the 'Spirit of Truth' and what He means to your daily relationship with Jesus.

3. End your time of study today in **prayer**.

Read John 14:25-31.

1. Based on John 14:27 what does the Spirit use to give us peace?

2. How does this calm a troubled heart?

3. In John 14:28, Jesus assured the disciples that they would see Him again. What does His return to the Father make possible for us? What else did Jesus tell us about His Father and how does this benefit us?

4. Read Hebrews 2:17-18 and Hebrews 4:14-16 to describe Jesus' intercessory ministry on our behalf.

5. In John 14:30-31, Jesus named two of our great spiritual enemies. List what those are and tell how being 'in Christ' benefits our daily lives from the footholds the enemy of Jesus may try to get in our lives. Tie this into what you have learned about the Holy Spirit so far.

6. The perfect peace of Jesus assures us that He alone gives true peace to us. Jesus is always the Master of all situations, and He enables us as we daily submit to Him through the power of our 'Comforter' and 'Spirit of Truth'. Close out this week of study by **praying through** any situation in your life that is currently affecting your peace. Give everything to Jesus, believing that He alone brings peace, comfort, and truth to you.

Blessing Your Spirit

_____, I bless your spirit in the name of Jesus. Listen to the Word of God for you. "For to us a child is born to us a son is given and the government will be on his shoulders. And he will be called Wonderful Counselor, Mighty God, Everlasting Father, Prince of Peace. Of the increase of His government there will be no end" (Isaiah 9:6-7).

_____, you are under the protection of God who can do the impossible. I bless you with peace that comes from God. I bless you with knowing that God makes peace regardless of your circumstances. Many circumstances that you will face in your life are not conducive to peace, but God decrees the light of His presence shines in this dark world.

I bless you with an anointing for taking the peace of the Lord Jesus Chris to those who do not know it, as an overflow of your life. When you walk in this peace, the peace of those around you will increase, even if they carry turmoil. I bless you with being known as someone who carries the peace of God with you everywhere you go, so that people will seek you out because they are so desperate for the peace of God.

I bless you, _____, with being a part of a community of faith that experiences the peace of God, that walks in a deep submission to the King of Kings and Lord of Lords and Prince of Peace—a fellowship that has learned to enthrone Jesus, so that their peace is pervasive, enough to bring peace to the world that is in darkness. I bless you, _____, with an intimate relationship with God who makes peace. I bless you with that peace in the name of Jesus.

Week Three

A Mighty Fortress is Our God

A mighty fortress is our God, a bulwark never failing;
Our helper He, amid the flood of mortal ills prevailing:
For still our ancient foe doth seek to work us woe;
His craft and pow'r are great, and, armed with cruel hate,
On earth is not his equal.

Did we in our own strength confide, our striving would be losing,
Were not the right Man on our side, the Man of God's own choosing:
Dost ask who that may be? Christ Jesus, it is He;
Lord Sabaoth, His Name, from age to age the same,
And He must win the battle.

And though this world, with devils filled, should threaten to undo us,
We will not fear, for God hath willed His truth to triumph through us;
The Prince of Darkness grim, we tremble not for him;
His rage we can endure, for lo, his doom is sure,
One little word shall fell him.

That word above all earthly pow'rs, no thanks to them, abideth;
The Spirit and the gifts are ours through Him Who with us sideth;
Let goods and kindred go, this mortal life also;
The body they may kill: God's truth abideth still,
His kingdom is forever.

Martin Luther, 1529, Public Domain

We live in a world that is hostile to Jesus and His Gospel message. Jesus openly taught His disciples that one day persecution would come. It was obvious throughout the gospel of John, that the religious establishment not only opposed Jesus, but even sought to kill Him. As Jesus continued His ministry, He encountered resentment, hatred, and ultimately open opposition.

Jesus knew all of this would affect the twelve disciples He had taught and Instructed for three years, so He spent quite a bit of time preparing them and letting them know that once He departed, He would send 'another Comforter'. Jesus knew we too would encounter not only hostility from the world as we live for Him, but we would also navigate trials and hardships of life.

These three chapters of John (John 14, 15, 16) contain the key message of Jesus about the Holy Spirit and His ministry in our lives. What is the secret of walking in victory in our lives? The presence and power of the Holy Spirit.

Re-read all of John 15 today.

1. This entire chapter of John is about relationships and responsibilities. Jesus used the images of branches and friends. Who is the True Vine?

2. Describe the relationship between the vine and the branches in verses 1-8. Tell the responsibility of each one.

3. Can the branch produce fruit on its own? Why or why not?

4. What is the key word in this passage (John 15:1-11) and what are the practical ways you can live out this key word? Write the definition of this word.

5. Close out this day of study by **praying to your True Vine** and declaring your fellowship with Him so that you continue to bear fruit.

Yesterday, we learned how the branch cannot produce its own life; it must draw that life from the vine. This is called 'abiding' or 'remaining' in the vine. It is our communion with Christ through the Holy Spirit that makes it possible for us to bear fruit.

The abiding relationship is natural to the branch and the vine, but it must be cultivated as we walk out the Christian life. It does not happen automatically. Abiding in Christ will mean that we worship, meditate on God's Word, pray, sacrifice, and serve.

In the second part of John 15, Jesus talked to His disciples as friends. He revealed a relationship of love, both for Him and for each other.

Read John 15:12-17 to answer the following questions.

1. How is it possible for Jesus to command us to love one another? Can true love be commanded? Define love as stated in John 15:12

2. The proof of love is shown through our actions, and as Jesus has stated in this passage, even to the extent of laying down our lives for Christ and for one another. Look up 1 John 3:16 and Romans 5:10 to explain more of what Jesus meant in verse 13.

3. In verse 14, Jesus plainly stated what His friends do. What is He talking about in this verse and how can you apply it in your life? Would you describe yourself as a friend of Jesus?

4. Tell how the empowering presence of the Holy Spirit enables you to obey Jesus on a daily basis.

5. Dr. Oswald Sanders once said, "Each of us is as close to God as we choose to be." Write out how you can intentionally get closer to God in the days ahead and put your thoughts in the form of a **prayer** here.

As branches, we have the privilege of sharing the life of Jesus and the responsibility of abiding. As friends, we have the privilege of knowing His will, and the responsibility of obeying.

Our communion with Christ through the Holy Spirit makes fruit-bearing possible. Today we will be exploring what the Bible has to say about our fruit-bearing for Jesus. A true branch, united with the vine, will always bear fruit.

Read John 15:12-17 for today.

1. In verses 15-16, Jesus summarizes for us what it means to be His friend. Based on your study so far, what is the purpose of your friendship with Jesus and how do you display this friendship?

2. Write out John 15:16 here in your favorite version or translation of the Bible.

3. How does a Christian bear fruit?

4. Read the passage on the fruit of the Spirit in Galatians 5:16-26. Summarize how a believer is to keep in step with the Spirit based on your reading.

5. List out the fruit of the Spirit and define each one, also giving a practical example of each.

> *"How, then, shall a Christian bear fruit? By efforts and struggles to obtain that which is freely given, by meditations on watchfulness, on prayer, on action, on temptation, and on dangers? No: there must be a full concentration of the thoughts and affections on Christ; a complete surrender of the whole being to Him; a constant looking to Him for grace. Christians in whom these dispositions are once firmly fixed go on calmly as the infant borne in the arms of its mother."* ~John McCarthy

6. Use this quote to close out your study time today and **pray about** anything in your life that may need surrendering to Jesus so that you are indeed keeping in step with the Spirit.

This final section of John 15 reveals two important themes: the world is opposed to the church, and the ministry of the Holy Spirit to and through the church.

Read John 15:18-27 to answer the questions.

1. Before we study this portion of John 15, it is important to remember just who the Holy Spirit is. The Holy Spirit of God is a person; Jesus referred to the Spirit as 'He'. List out the three additional aspects of the Holy Spirit gleaned from these verses:

    *   Romans 8:27

    *   1 Corinthians 12:11

    *   Galatians 5:22-23

2. In John 15:18, Jesus made a very strong statement to us. Write out what Jesus said here:

3. Jesus gave us several reasons why the world system hates the Christian. List out what these reasons are according to these verses: John 15:18, 19, 21, and 22-24.

4. How does the Holy Spirit encourage believers when they are experiencing opposition? Use these passages to answer the question: 2 Timothy 2:9-12; Hebrews 12:3-4; 1 Peter 4:12.

> *"But when the Helper (Comforter, Advocate, Intercessor, Counselor, Strengthener, Standby) comes, whom I will send to you from the Father, that is the Spirit of Truth who comes from the Father, He will testify and bear witness about Me"*
> John 15:26 AMP.

5. Use this verse to vocalize your **prayer and praise** back to God as you process what you have gleaned from His Word in today's study.

Today we wrap up our study of John 15. Read the final verses in the Amplified version below and answer the questions.

> *"But when the Helper (Comforter, Advocate, Intercessor, Counselor, Strengthener, Standby) comes, whom I will send to you from the Father, that is the Spirit of Truth who comes from the Father, He will testify and bear witness about Me. But you will testify also and be My witnesses, because you have been with Me from the beginning"* John 15:26-27.

1. How many Persons of the Godhead (Trinity) are mentioned in this verse? Write them each out here.

2. Write out the truth of Galatians 2:20 here.

3. Because the Holy Spirit is a person and is God, this means the Christian has God indwelling her body! This is an incredible theological fact of Scripture. Look up the following verses and tell how the Holy Spirit enables us in each verse:

    -   Galatians 5:16

    -   Philippians 3:3

    -   Acts 1:8

4. Take the time today to review all of your lessons in John 15. Write the most meaningful ones here and put them in the form of **a prayer**.

Blessing Your Spirit

_____, listen with your spirit to the Word of God for you. "Peace I leave with you; my peace I give you. I do not give to you as the world gives. Do not let your hearts be troubled and do not be afraid" (John 14:27).

Jesus gave His peace to the disciples before He left His earthly relationship with them and returned to heaven. His peace which was transferred to them had various aspects. First there was a profound relationship with His Father which gave Him legitimacy in everything He did. It did not matter to Jesus that other people did not understand Him or that they opposed Him None of that affected His absolute certainty of who He was and His significance, because He had a relationship with His Father. He knew what His Father wanted Him to do, and He did it. There was nothing that could damage His relationship with His Father.

So, _____, I bless you with that kind of peace. I bless you with knowing deep in your spirit that God your Father's favor is upon you, that He loves you, likes you, enjoys you, and takes pleasure in who you are today, regardless of what you do. He finds pleasure in you while you sleep and when you wake up. I bless you with profoundly knowing that reality. I bless you with knowing your Father's love, with being secure, and having the peace of Jesus in your relationship with your Father.

_____, I bless you with the same sense of adequacy and assurance Jesus had, that each day will be Father-filtered, and that God Himself will see to it that nothing comes into your life that is beyond what His strength in you can handle.

I bless you with understanding in your spirit what your Father has called you to do, with a clear sense of the call of God on your life: the big picture as well as a daily sense of what God would have you do.

I bless you, _____, with the peace that Jesus had which is beyond what the world gives.

The Comforter

Week Four

Holy Spirit You Are Welcome Here

There is nothing worth more
That will ever come close
No thing can compare
You're our living hope
Your presence Lord

I've tasted and seen
Of the sweetest of love
When my heart becomes free
And my shame is undone
Your presence Lord

Holy Spirit, You are welcome here
Come flood this place and fill the atmosphere
Your glory, God, is what our hearts long for
To be overcome by Your presence, Lord

Holy Spirit, You are welcome here
Come flood this place and fill the atmosphere
Your glory, God, is what our hearts long for
To be overcome by Your presence, Lord

Let us become more aware of Your presence
Let us experience the glory of Your goodness

Holy Spirit, You are welcome here
Come flood this place and fill the atmosphere
Your glory, God, is what our hearts long for
To be overcome by Your presence, Lord

Katie and Bryan Torwalt—for noncommercial use only

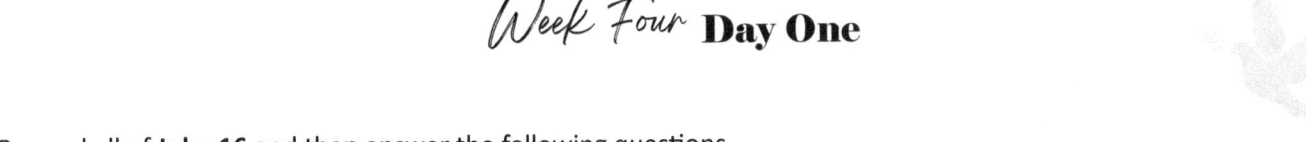

Re-read all of **John 16** and then answer the following questions.

1. In John 16:1-4, what did Jesus warn the disciples about?

2. In verses 5-6, what did Jesus specifically tell the disciples would happen? How did Jesus say they would emotionally respond?

> *"To the disciples, it must have seemed as if they were facing the end of their wonderful encounter with the Lord and with the power of God. Living and walking with Jesus was more than they had ever hoped for in this world. With Him (Jesus) at their side, their lives had been filled with adventure, excitement, joy, victory, power, healings, and miracles. What would life be without Jesus? Would it ever be the same? Was this the end of their dream?"* (page 44, Jesus Made a Promise, Rick Renner)

3. Read John 16:7-15 and list out the specific things Jesus said the "Helper" would do. Take your time with this as you unpack each verse.

4. ***Personal prayer time:*** take the time to talk with the Lord about what you have read, what you have learned, and perhaps any area in your own life where you need the Holy Spirit to highlight or bring more of into your life.

Jesus promised the Holy Spirit to His disciples. The Holy Spirit and His mission for the church have never changed.

The good news is the Holy Spirit has come to teach us and to provide wisdom for us as we listen to Him and cooperate with Him.

Read John 16:7-15 again for today's questions.

1. Write out John 16:7 and explain why Jesus had to go away and why it was for the advantage of the disciples.

2. The major reason the Holy Spirit was sent (poured out) after Jesus ascended to heaven was to empower the church (believers) for life and witness. Write out what Jesus said the Holy Spirit would do (verses 8-11) when He came.

3. Using what you have learned from your study so far and these verses in John 16, what is the primary job of the Holy Spirit through the surrendered lives of believers?

4. Compare John 14:26 with John 16:13, and explain the wonderful way that God arranged for the writing of the New Testament.

5. Use your **private prayer** time to praise God for His precious Holy Spirit.

The final portion of John 16 concludes Jesus' discussion in the Upper Room with His disciples. Jesus dealt with the emotions of the men as they were sad, confused, and afraid. They had been told Jesus was leaving them and they were unsure as to what that meant for the days ahead.

Oh, how they would need the Holy Spirit!

Read John 16:16-22 to answer the questions.

1. What did Jesus announce to the disciples in verse 16?

2. Verses 17-18 reveal the reaction of the disciples to Jesus' announcement. Describe their reaction and tell how this can encourage you as you read and study your Bible when you find things that you do not understand.

3. In verses 19-22, Jesus explains to the disciples again what would happen. What is the theme of Jesus' message to the disciples?

4. Perhaps today you are personally dealing with grief or disappointment. Jesus understands your emotions and He promises as you turn to Him, you will discover His joy. His Holy Spirit is your Counselor, Advocate, Intercessor, Helper and Friend. Spend a few minutes **praying today** based on what you have studied.

The last portion of Jesus' conversation with the disciples is filled with the promises of prayer.

Read John 16:23-28 to answer the questions.

1. In John 16:23, Jesus refers to a specific time. What time was He referring to? Refer back to John 16:22 to answer and see also Acts 1:3.

2. Jesus mentioned prayer many times in His ministry, and He set the example for prayer in His own life. He was a Man of Prayer. In this time of conversation in the Upper Room, Jesus emphasized prayer and made it clear that believing prayer is one of the most important aspects of a fruitful Christian life. Look up the following scriptures and write the lessons learned from what Jesus had to say about prayer:

   • John 14:12-14

   • John 15:7

   • John 15:16

   • John 16:23-26

3. What does it mean to ask for something in prayer in Jesus' name?

4. In John 16:25-27, Jesus explained that there would be a new situation emerging because of His resurrection and ascension to heaven, and because of the coming Holy Spirit. Jesus would no longer speak with them in ways that required spiritual insight for their understanding. Explain how Jesus would speak to them in the future based on these verses.

5. In our study of these specific chapters of John, we have seen Jesus use symbolic images to explain his message: *the Father's house, the vine and the branches, the birth of a baby.* In the days that would follow, these images would become more clear to the disciples as they would be taught by the Holy Spirit. Using John 16:25 and what you have gleaned so far from this study, explain the purpose of Bible study.

6. Look up the following verses and write each one out here:

   • Romans 8:34

   • Hebrews 7:25

   • 1 John 2:1

7. Based on your study of prayer today, write out your **personal prayer** here, thanking Jesus for His joy and transforming power and victory through prayer.

The last few verses of John 16 reflect a turning point in the disciples' understanding.

Read John 16:29-33 and answer the questions.

1. In verse 29, what did the disciples claim and say to Jesus?

2. In verse 30, write out the disciples' declaration of faith.

3. In verses 31-32, Jesus issued a warning for His disciples. What was it?

4. Jesus has promised never to leave us alone. Write out the following promises of Scripture here:

    •   Matthew 28:20

    •   Hebrews 13:5

5. John 16:33 is the summary and high point of Jesus' message to his friends in the Upper Room. Write out the message here and tell why He gave this message.

6. Summarize what you have learned from John 16 and put your findings in a personal **prayer here.** This is truly your response to everything Jesus taught about the purpose of His life, death, resurrection, and now living in us through the power of the Holy Spirit. Be of good cheer, Jesus has overcome the world!! Praise God for His overcoming power in your life!

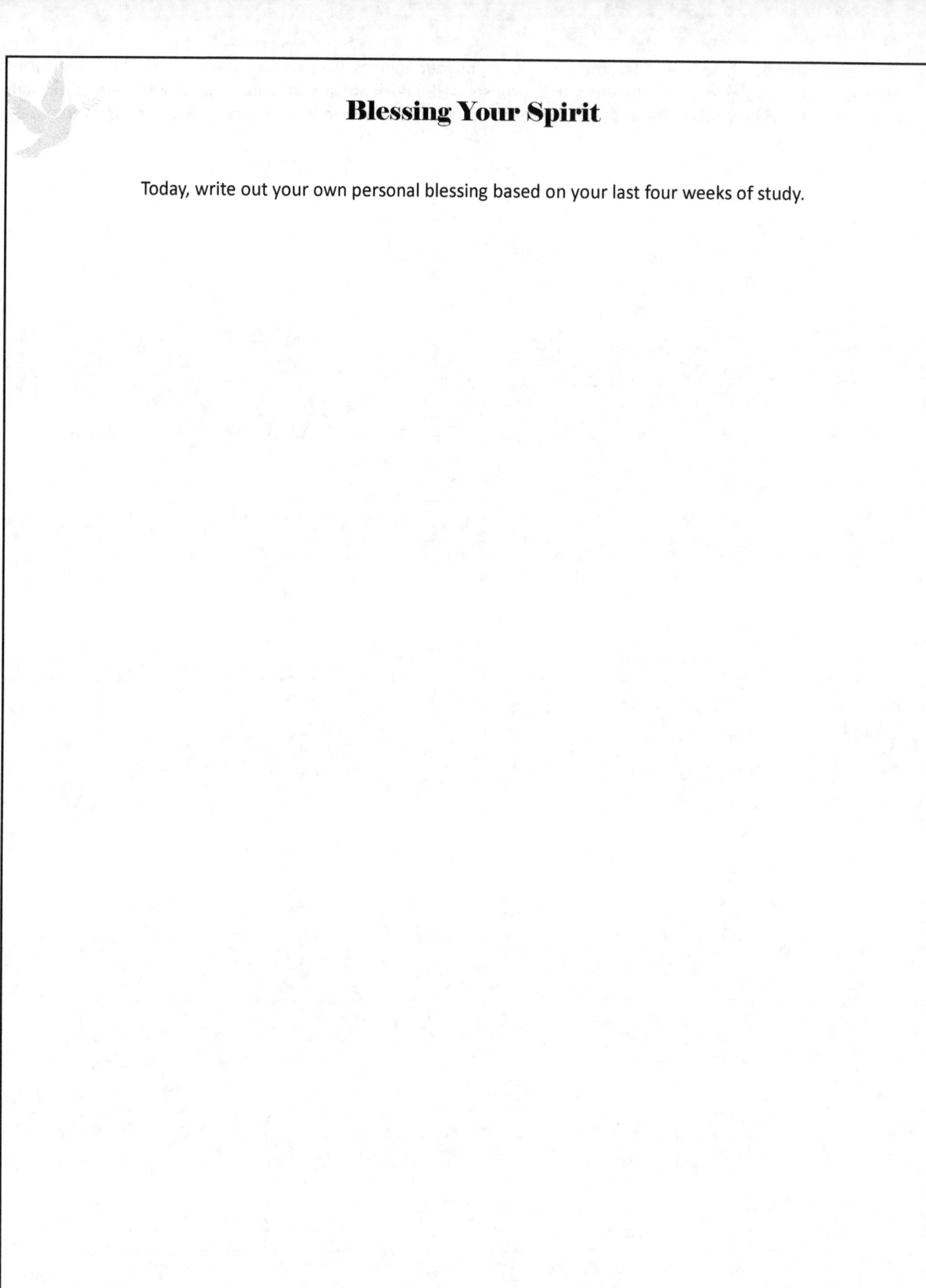

Blessing Your Spirit

Today, write out your own personal blessing based on your last four weeks of study.

Week Five

Spirit of the Living God

Spirit of the Living God,
Fall afresh on me,
Spirit of the Living God,
Fall afresh on me.
Break me, melt me, mold me, fill me.
Spirit of the Living God,
Fall afresh on me.

Yes, Lord!: Church of God in Christ hymnal #197

You have spent the last four weeks unpacking the three chapters of John's gospel where Jesus' personal message about the Holy Spirit was given to the disciples. We could spend our entire lives studying the Holy Spirit and still have more to learn!

This final chapter is a study on the biblical truth revealed about the Holy Spirit.

If anyone understood the partnership of the Holy Spirit, it was the Lord Jesus Christ. His earthly ministry was completely dependent on the Holy Spirit.

From the time of His birth onward, everything in His life was in alignment with divine purpose and the power of the Holy Spirit.

1. Look up each Scripture and write out the important facts revealed about the Holy Spirit.

    *   Matthew 1:18, 20; Luke 1:35

    *   Luke 1:41-45

    *   Luke 2:25-38

    *   Matthew 3:11; Luke 3:16; John 1:33; Acts 11:16

2. Write down anything you saw from these scriptures that impacted you in a fresh way.

We will continue our journey of the facts about the Holy Spirit in the scriptures provided.

1. Jesus spoke of the baptism of the Holy Spirit. Write out His specific instructions found in Luke 24:49 and Acts 1:4,5.

2. Write out the facts about Jesus' water baptism from these verses: Matthew 3:16; Mark 1:10; Luke 3:22; John 1:32.

3. What do you see about the fullness of the Spirit from John 3:34?

4. What do you learn about the Holy Spirit's leading from Matthew 4:1; Mark 1:12; Luke 4:1?

Each of the scripture verses for today reveal more biblical truth about the Holy Spirit.

1. Describe what occurred when Jesus returned to Galilee as told in Luke 4:14.

2. What did Jesus state publicly about His ministry as seen in Luke 4:18?

3. Look up the following Scriptures and tell what Jesus taught about the ministry of the Holy Spirit:

    *   Matthew 10:20

    *   Mark 13:11

    *   Luke 11:13

    *   Luke 12:12

    *   John 7:39

4. What did Jesus proclaim in John 3:5-8?

Jesus and the Holy Spirit were in divine partnership in order to accomplish Jesus' divine role on the earth.

As we wrap up our biblical search of the facts, look up each scripture reference and answer the questions.

1. Describe the Lamb of God as stated in Hebrews 9:14.

2. How was Jesus resurrected from the dead as written in Romans 8:11?

3. What did Jesus do to the disciples after His resurrection? See John 20:22 to answer.

4. Read all of Acts 2 and tell the current position of Jesus and what was poured out on the church. What was the result of Peter's sermon?

5. How did Jesus instruct the disciples? Use Acts 1:2 to answer.

Review and worship!

Use the time today to review any area of your last five weeks of Bible study that you want to focus on again.

Re-visit your personal written prayers throughout your days of study and take time in prayer to talk with the Lord about anything new that is on your heart.

Use this time to worship the Lord in praise and gratitude. Sing the songs and hymns provided for you in your study book.

Complete your study by writing out the most meaningful aspects of the Holy Spirit for you personally throughout this time.

How will you be different as a result of this study?

Works Cited

The Amplified Bible, Grand Rapids, MI: Zondervan Bible, 1983. Print.

Burk, Arthur. Gunter, Sylvia. *Blessing Your Spirit.* Birmingham, AL: The Father's Business. 2005. Print.

Renner Rick. *The Holy Spirit and You!* Tulsa, OK: Harrison House. 2017. Print.

Stanley, Charles. *The Wonderful Spirit-filled Life.* Nashville, TN: Thomas Nelson Publishers. 1992. Print.

Wiersbe, Warren. *The Wiersbe Bible Commentary.* Colorado Springs, CO: David C. Cook. 2007. Print.

About the Author

Marjie Schaefer was born in Georgia, raised in Texas and has spent the past four decades in Washington state. She and her husband, Steve, have been married for 37 years and have four grown children and two grandchildren.

Marjie describes herself as an everyday girl who loves Jesus and daily pursues a life with Him at the center of her activities and purposes.

She started leading and teaching Bible studies while a student at Washington State University and has continued to open her home and her life to anyone who wants more of the Word and more of Jesus. Her greatest passion is bringing the Word of God to life through practical application and visual tools. Women look forward to her personal touches while attending her studies, and they usually go home with tangible reminders of God's love for them.

Marjie started spending deliberate and daily time in the Word of God while she was a young girl at the encouragement of her godly mother. This has given her a foundation that has stood the test of time. She began writing her own Bible studies at the request of some friends who desired to study the Word during the summer months.

Marjie and her team currently lead the ministry, **Flourish Through the Word,** a 501c3 non-profit organization which is a community of women in the greater Seattle region committed to being equipped through God's Word. As a result of their time together in God's Word, women move out into their arenas of influence, shining their light for Jesus.

Please visit _www.flourishthroughtheword.com_ to find out more about Bible studies available for you or your church, along with various upcoming events.

www.ingramcontent.com/pod-product-compliance
Lightning Source LLC
Chambersburg PA
CBHW080856120626
46553CB00009B/2651